Volcano
TREK

Rob Waring, *Series Editor*

HEINLE
CENGAGE Learning™

Australia • Brazil • Japan • Korea • Mexico • Singapore • Spain • United Kingdom • United States

Words to Know

This story is set in Africa, in the country of Ethiopia. It happens in the Afar (afar) region near a volcano called Erta Ale (ɜrtə ɑlə).

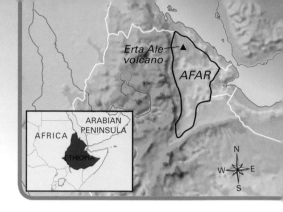

A **A Volcano.** Read the paragraph. Then, label the picture with the underlined words.

A volcano is a mountain with a large hole at the top. This hole is called a crater. In an eruption, a volcano produces very hot, melted rock. When it is under the ground, this hot, melted rock is called magma. Once it comes out of the volcano, the hot rock is called lava. Sometimes lava comes together in the crater. This is called a lava lake.

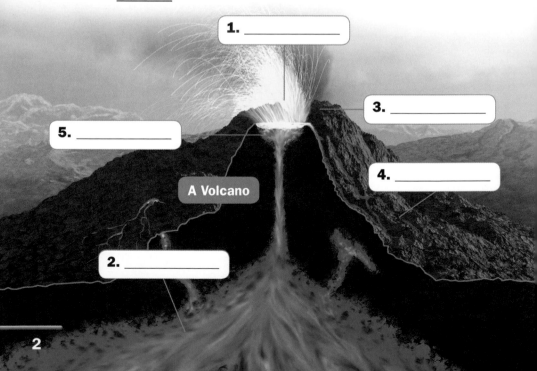

1. _____

3. _____

5. _____

4. _____

A Volcano

2. _____

B Volcano Explorers. Read the paragraph. Then, match each word with the correct definition.

This story is about two explorers from Nice (nis), France, Franck Tessier (fraŋk tɛsyeɪ) and Irene Margaritis (aɪrin mɑrgəritɪs). These explorers are geologists who are trekking to the Erta Ale volcano. They ride camels to get to the volcano because it is difficult to reach it. Volcanoes can be dangerous. The geologists want to study the volcano's lava, rocks, and soil. They want to learn more about volcanoes and how they work. This information may help people and save lives.

1. explorers _____
2. geologists _____
3. trek _____
4. camels _____
5. dangerous _____

a. make a long, difficult journey
b. scientists who study Earth
c. not safe
d. large animals that often carry people or things
e. people who travel to new places to learn new things

The Earth

Rocks and Soil

Millions of years ago, **man's earliest ancestors**[1] lived in Africa, in a far region of Ethiopia. Here in this area is the Erta Ale volcano. Hot lava has erupted from this volcano for about one hundred years. The temperature of the lava here is more than **2,000 degrees Fahrenheit.**[2]

Now, a team of explorers is going to explore Erta Ale for themselves. They want to learn more about the volcano. However, it's not an easy trek, and the team has to use camels to get to the area. The camels are able to carry the team and the heavy things they need for their research.

---

[1]**man's earliest ancestors:** some of the first people on Earth
[2]**2,000 degrees Fahrenheit:** 1093° (degrees) Celsius

CD 3, Track 09

The explorers and their camels finally reach the crater of the Erta Ale volcano. Franck Tessier and Irene Margaritis are **professors**[3] at the University of Nice in France. They're geologists, or scientists who study the earth. They have traveled halfway around the world just to see the Erta Ale volcano. They are hoping that they'll find something very interesting. They want to find data that will tell them about the history of Earth.

---

[3]**professor:** teacher at a university or college

The geologists look down into the volcano. Deep in the crater, they can see the black lava lake of Erta Ale. Professor Margaritis is very happy to finally be here. "It is quite **exciting**.[4] I want to see it now," she says. Very soon, they will go into the crater and look at the lava more closely. But why is the Erta Ale volcano so special for geologists?

---

[4]**exciting:** causing a very happy feeling

Infer Meaning

1. Why is Professor Margaritis happy?

2. What does she mean by 'it' in "I want to see it now"?

The Erta Ale volcano is in the Afar area of Ethiopia. The Afar **triangle**[5] is in an area where three **continental plates**[6] meet. These plates move farther and farther apart every year. Because of this, it's an area that's always changing.

Erta Ale has the oldest lava lake in the world. The lake is also one of the lowest points on Earth. At Erta Ale, geologists can study how the world began millions of years ago. That's why this place is so special.

─────────────────────────

[5]**triangle:** an area with three sides
[6]**continental plates:** geologist's term for the large pieces of rock far under the ground

Continental Plates

Afar Triangle

A lava lake is a mixture of hot and cooler lava. Very hot lava comes out of the earth. This lava forms the base of Erta Ale's lava lake. As this lava **cools down**,[7] it becomes hard and black. However, a lava lake is a place of change and movement. Soon, hot magma breaks through this covering as the volcano erupts again and again. Erta Ale is an active volcano and it's fair to say that it could have a big eruption at almost any time!

---

[7]**cools down:** becomes cold

The geologists stand at the top of this active volcano and wait at the side of the crater. It's very interesting for them, but it's not easy to be here. There's a very strong smell of **sulfur**[8] in the air. And even in the early morning, it's already very, very hot.

It soon gets even hotter as the group goes slowly and carefully down into the crater. Professor Tessier wants to collect **samples**[9] of the red-hot lava near the lava lake. The team spends many hours down by the lake.

_____

[8]**sulfur:** a yellow material that smells very bad
[9]**sample:** a small amount

It's a very long day for the geologists. In fact, it's two o'clock in the morning when they return from the crater. They have all worked very hard. Professor Margaritis has only one thing to say about the trek; "very hot," she says with a smile.

Everyone is pleased with the lava samples the team brings back from the crater. "I think this is **fresh**[10] lava," Tessier says about his samples. He then explains to the team that the pieces didn't come directly from the lava lake. However, the team decides the samples are fresh enough and they put them in a bag. The geologists will analyze these samples later.

---

[10] **fresh:** new

After a difficult trek, the team finally has their samples of lava. They will now leave Erta Ale and go back to study the lava. What do they want to learn? As professors, Margaritis and Tessier want to learn new information that they can teach to others. However, as geologists, they also want to know what the lava of Erta Ale may teach them. The lava may help them to understand more about Erta Ale, about volcanoes in general, and about how the world began millions of years ago.

Summarize

Summarize the story of the volcano trek. Tell it to a partner or write it in a notebook. Include the following information:

- Who went on the trek?
- What did they want to see?
- Where did they go?
- Why did they want to go there?

After You Read

1. Hot lava has erupted from Erta Ale for how many years?
    A. millions of years
    B. about 100 years
    C. more than 2,000 years
    D. 1,000,000 years

2. Why does the team use camels to get to the volcano?
    A. Camels like volcanoes.
    B. Camels can reach 2,000 degrees Fahrenheit.
    C. Camels are fast animals.
    D. Camels can carry many things.

3. On page 7, what data does the team want to collect?
    A. data about the history of the earth
    B. data about the temperature of the volcano
    C. data about how long the volcano has been erupting
    D. data on all of the above

4. Professor Margaritis is _____ excited about being at the lava lake.
    A. a little
    B. very
    C. not
    D. never

5. What is the writer's purpose on page 10?
    A. to show that Erta Ale is in a triangle
    B. to teach about Ethiopia's towns
    C. to tell more about the Erta Ale volcano
    D. to teach why the continental plates are moving together

6. What is a good heading for page 12?
    A. Lava Lakes Made from Cool Lava
    B. Erta Ale Is a Safe Volcano.
    C. How a Lava Lake Forms.
    D. A Long, Hot Trek to the Crater

7. Which does NOT happen at the Erta Ale volcano?
   A. Cool magma makes a lava lake.
   B. Lava comes out from deep in the earth.
   C. Lava cools down.
   D. Hot magma erupts again and again.

8. What does 'collect' mean on page 14?
   A. see
   B. bring
   C. get
   D. touch

9. Which is NOT a good heading for page 16?
   A. 2:00 a.m. Return from Volcano
   B. Geologists Go Down into Crater
   C. Tired Professors Worked Hard
   D. Hot Trek Makes Explorers Tired

10. When the team decides the samples are 'fresh enough,' they mean that they're:
   A. old
   B. not acceptable
   C. cold
   D. OK to use

11. The explorers are excited to _____ from and _____ about the lava.
   A. know, study
   B. taught, studied
   C. learn, teach
   D. teach, teach

MAN VS. VOLCANO:
Can there be a winner?

Scientists tell us that the earth currently has about seventy active volcanoes. Right now, there are probably about twenty volcanic eruptions happening in the world. Some of these eruptions are large and some are very small, but all of them can be deadly.

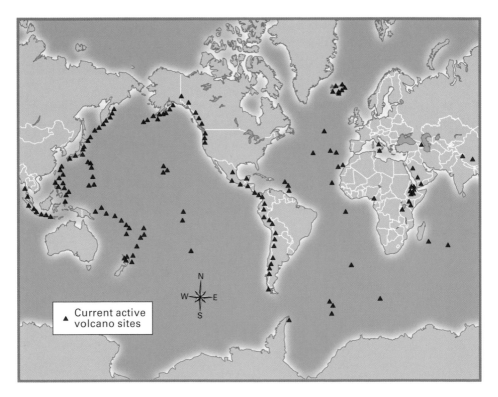

Current active volcano sites

A Map of Current Active Volcano Sites

The number of people on Earth is increasing. As a result, people often find themselves living in dangerous areas near volcanoes. Over three million people live near Mount Rainer in the U.S. Another one million people live near Mount Etna in Sicily, Italy. It is quite possible that either of these areas may experience a volcanic eruption in the future.

For centuries, scientists have tried different ways of protecting people from volcanoes. They have tried:

- Stopping the eruption
  (This was impossible.)

- Forcing the lava to move away from where people live
  (This was difficult to do.)

- Asking people not to live near volcanoes (This has not worked.)

- Making plans for people to leave the area of an eruption quickly
  (This sometimes works.)

None of these ideas were particularly effective.

Geologists are now trying to find new ways to know when a volcano is going to erupt. They know that most volcanic activity happens near the sides of continental plates. These plates are always coming together or moving away from one another. When a lot of magma pushes up under moving plates, we often see a volcanic eruption. Geologists also know that before the eruption happens, something called 'lahar' starts moving under the ground. Lahar is made from hot water, magma and pieces of stone. Geologists are now using a machine that is placed under the ground. This machine keeps a record of the movement of the lahar. When there are a lot of quick movements, scientists know that an eruption is likely to happen.

CD 3, Track 10

Word Count: 302
Time: _____

Vocabulary List

camel (3, 4, 7)

continental plate (10)

cool down (12)

crater (2, 7, 8, 14, 16)

dangerous (3)

eruption (2, 12)

exciting (8)

explorer (3, 4, 7)

fresh (16)

geologist (3, 7, 8, 10, 14, 16, 19)

lava (2, 4, 8, 12, 14, 16, 19)

lava lake (2, 8, 10, 12, 14)

magma (2, 12)

man's earliest ancestors (4)

professor (7, 8, 9, 14, 16, 19)

sample (14, 16, 19)

sulfur (14)

trek (3, 4, 19)

triangle (10)